FOOTBALL FUEL

RECIPES FOR BEFORE, DURING, AND AFTER THE BIG GAME

by Katrina Jorgensen

CAPSTONE PRESS
a capstone imprint

Sports Illustrated Kids Football Cookbooks are published by Capstone Press,
1710 Roe Crest Drive, North Mankato, Minnesota 56003.
www.capstonepub.com

Sports Illustrated Kids is a trademark of Time Inc. Used with permission.

Library of Congress Cataloging-in-Publication Data
Jorgensen, Katrina, author.
  Football fuel : recipes for before, during, and after the big game /
by Katrina Jorgensen.
      pages cm.—(Sports illustrated kids. Football cookbooks)
  Summary: "A fun cookbook with recipes aimed to prepare student athletes for a
game, as well as provide nutritious options during and after the game"—Provided
by publisher.
  Audience: Ages 9-15.
  Audience: Grades 4 to 6.
  Includes bibliographical references.
  ISBN 978-1-4914-2135-2 (library binding)
1. Cooking—Juvenile literature. 2. Football players—Nutrition—Juvenile literature.
3. Physical fitness—Juvenile literature. I. Title.
  TX652.5.J67 2015
  641.5'6—dc23   2014034064

Editorial Credits
Anthony Wacholtz, editor; Kyle Grenz, designer; Eric Gohl, media researcher;
Laura Manthe, production specialist; Marcy Morin, scheduler; Sarah Schuette,
food stylist

Photo Credits
All images by Capstone Studio: Karon Dubke; author photo by
STILLCODA Photography.

The author dedicates this book to Jennie and Ben for lending their
taste buds during the research process.

Printed in Canada.
092014   008478FRS15

TABLE OF CONTENTS

The Day of the Big Game

Pack your gear and run for the end zone! It's time to fuel up for the big game. These recipes will keep your mind and body in peak condition so you can make the perfect pass, dive into the end zone, or make a drive-ending tackle. The recipes in this book follow the day of a football player. Use the table of contents on page 3 to help you plan out the food you'll need to be a star player.

COOKING 101

PREP TIME — the amount of time it takes to prepare ingredients before cooking

INACTIVE PREP TIME — the amount of time it takes to indirectly prepare ingredients before cooking, such as allowing dough to rise

COOK TIME — the amount of time it takes to cook a recipe after preparing the ingredients

Conversions

Using metric tools? No problem! Here are measurement conversions to make your recipe measure up.

Temperature

Fahrenheit	Celsius
325°	160°
350°	180°
375°	190°
400°	200°
425°	220°
450°	230°

Measurements

1⁄4 teaspoon	1.25 grams or milliliters
1⁄2 teaspoon	2.5 g or mL
1 teaspoon	5 g or mL
1 tablespoon	15 g or mL
1⁄4 cup	57 g (dry) or 60 mL (liquid)
1⁄3 cup	75 g (dry) or 80 mL (liquid)
1⁄2 cup	114 g (dry) or 125 mL (liquid)
2⁄3 cup	150 g (dry) or 160 mL (liquid)
3⁄4 cup	170 g (dry) or 175 mL (liquid)
1 cup	227 g (dry) or 240 mL (liquid)
1 quart	950 mL

blend—to mix together, sometimes using a blender

boil—to heat until large bubbles form on top of a liquid; the boiling point for water is 212°F (100°C)

chop—to cut into small pieces with a knife

dissolve—to incorporate a solid food into a liquid by melting or stirring

grate—to cut into small strips using a grater

knead—to mix dough by flattening it with the heel of your hand, folding it in half, pressing down again, and repeating several times; use flour on your work surface to prevent the dough from sticking

mash—to smash a soft food into a lumpy mixture

preheat—to turn the oven on ahead of time so it reaches the correct temperature before you are ready to bake

simmer—to cook foods in hot liquids kept just below the boiling point of water

slice—to cut into thin pieces with a knife

spread—to put a thin layer of a soft food onto another food

thaw—to bring frozen food to room temperature

Keep your eye open for helpful, creative, and informative sidebars throughout the book. Switch up your recipes with Call an Audible ideas, and get insight from the expert with Coach's Tips. Athlete Nutrition highlights valuable nutrient information to explain why certain foods are good for you—the athlete.

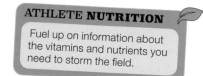

CALL AN AUDIBLE

Not liking what you see at the start of the play? Make some changes in the recipe to have success against even the toughest defenses.

COACH'S TIP

Gain the edge in the kitchen with these cool tips, tricks, and techniques.

ATHLETE NUTRITION

Fuel up on information about the vitamins and nutrients you need to storm the field.

Safety in the Kitchen

You can have fun in the kitchen and be safe too. Always start your recipes with clean hands, tools, and surfaces. Make sure you wash your hands and keep your tools and surfaces clean after handling raw meat. Use your knife carefully. Ask an adult for help when cutting food or handling hot dishes.

Just as football players need the right equipment to play their best, you'll need a variety of tools to tackle these recipes.

1. baking dish
2. baking sheets
3. can opener
4. chef's knife
5. colander
6. cutting board
7. grater
8. kitchen shears
9. large skillet
10. 2-inch ice cream scoop
11. measuring cups
12. measuring spoons
13. mixing bowls
14. mixing spoon
15. pastry brush
16. pizza cutter
17. rolling pin
18. slotted spoon
19. spatula
20. tongs
21. whisk

MAPLE NUT GRANOLA CEREAL

It's the day of the big game! Although the kickoff doesn't happen for hours, you'll want to start fueling your body in the morning. Start off by making granola with a maple-nut crunch. You can eat it as cereal with milk or mix it with yogurt.

PREP TIME	**10** MINUTES
COOK TIME	**45** MINUTES
MAKES	**8 TO 10** SERVINGS

Tools

- baking sheet
- parchment paper
- mixing bowl
- measuring cups/spoons
- spoon

Ingredients

- 2 cups rolled oats
- ½ cup walnuts, chopped
- ⅓ cup ground flaxseed
- ½ cup raisins
- ½ cup pure maple syrup
- ⅓ cup olive oil
- 2 teaspoons maple extract
- ⅛ teaspoon salt

1 Preheat oven to 300°F and line a baking sheet with parchment paper and set aside.

2 In a mixing bowl, combine the oats, walnuts, flaxseed, and raisins.

3 Add the remaining ingredients. Gently stir until the oats are well coated.

4 Spread the mixture evenly on the baking sheet.

5 Bake for about 45 minutes or until slightly browned.

6 Allow to cool completely, then break into chunks.

7 Store leftovers in an airtight container for up to two weeks.

ATHLETE NUTRITION

Go nuts over the walnuts in this cereal! Not only are they tasty, but they provide all-important iron. This essential mineral helps carry oxygen in your blood and to your muscles.

COACH'S TIP

Have fun with your granola! Spread 2 tablespoons peanut butter on a slice of apple for a tasty treat. Then sprinkle granola on top.

PUMPKIN WAFFLE SANDWICH

Ready for a breakfast sandwich that will help you keep your eyes on the ball? Pumpkin contains plenty of vitamin A to keep your vision sharp on the field.

PREP TIME 10 MINUTES

COOK TIME 5 MINUTES

MAKES 4 WAFFLE SANDWICHES

Ingredients

- ½ cup all-purpose flour
- 1 teaspoon baking powder
- 1 teaspoon pumpkin pie spice
- 1 pinch salt
- 1 egg
- 3 tablespoons pure maple syrup
- ¼ cup canned pureed pumpkin
- ½ cup milk
- 1 tablespoon canola oil
- cooking spray

For the filling:

- 3 tablespoons cream cheese, softened to room temperature
- ½ teaspoon maple extract

Tools

- 3 mixing bowls
- measuring cups/ spoons
- whisk
- waffle iron
- tongs
- spoon
- knife

1 In a mixing bowl, combine the dry ingredients: flour, baking powder, pumpkin pie spice, and salt.

2 In a second mixing bowl, whisk the wet ingredients: egg, syrup, pumpkin, milk, and canola oil until smooth.

3 Gently add the wet ingredients to the dry ingredients. Stir to combine.

4 Heat a waffle iron, and spritz with cooking spray.

CALL AN AUDIBLE

If your taste buds are blowing the whistle on pumpkin, try a mashed banana instead.

5 Pour half the batter on the iron. Cook according to the waffle iron directions or until golden brown and slightly crispy on the outside.

6 Remove from the iron using tongs and repeat with the second half of the batter.

7 For the filling, combine the cream cheese and maple extract in a small mixing bowl and stir until smooth.

8 When both of the waffles are done, spread the cream cheese on one of the waffles and place the second on top to make a sandwich.

9 Cut into quarters and serve.

SCRAMBLED EGG MUFFINS

After a game or workout, protein helps build and repair your muscles. Lucky for you, these muffins have scrambled eggs, which are high in protein!

PREP TIME	10 MINUTES
COOK TIME	20 MINUTES
MAKES	4 EGG MUFFINS

Ingredients

- cooking spray
- 2 eggs
- ¼ cup milk
- 1 pinch salt
- 1 pinch black pepper
- 2 slices deli ham
- ½ red bell pepper
- ¼ cup grated cheddar or Swiss cheese

Tools

- muffin tin
- mixing bowl
- whisk
- chef's knife
- cutting board

1 Preheat oven to 350°F. Spritz cooking spray in four cups of a standard muffin tin and set aside.

2 Beat the eggs, milk, salt, and pepper in a mixing bowl and set aside.

3 Dice the ham and red pepper into small pieces.

4 Add the cheese, ham, and red pepper to the eggs and mix.

5 Evenly pour the mixture into the muffin cups.

6 Bake for about 20 minutes or until the eggs are cooked through. The eggs are done when they are slightly firm but not hard.

7 Cool for about 5 minutes before serving.

CALL AN AUDIBLE

Vegetarians can eject ham from the recipe and put in some of their favorite veggies. Try the recipe with mushrooms, zucchini, or onions.

COACH'S TIP

It will take some practice to cut a bell pepper correctly, but follow these tips and you'll get it down in no time. First cut the pepper on top to remove the stem. Then cut it in half lengthwise, from stem to bottom. Scoop out the seeds and pith (the white fibrous veins running up and down the pepper). Then you're set to cut it into the sizes you need!

APPLE-CRANBERRY OATMEAL

This easy and delicious oatmeal provides your body with plenty of complex carbohydrates. They are a great source of long-lasting energy for your game day!

PREP TIME | 10 MINUTES

COOK TIME | 10 MINUTES

MAKES | 1 SERVING

Tools
- cutting board
- chef's knife
- saucepan
- spoon

Ingredients
- 1 apple
- 1 cup rolled oats
- 2 cups milk
- 3 tablespoons dried cranberries
- 2 tablespoons pure honey

1 Dice the apple into bite-sized pieces and set aside.

2 In a small saucepan, combine the oats and milk and place on a stovetop at medium heat.

3 Bring to a simmer and stir frequently.

4 As the oats soften, add the apple, cranberries, and honey.

5 Continue to stir for about 5 minutes. Serve warm.

CALL AN AUDIBLE

Add more toppings to your oatmeal. Toss in some chopped nuts for added crunch and flavor. You can also combine recipes by adding some Maple Nut Granola Cereal from page 8.

What are complex carbohydrates and why are they good for your body? Complex carbohydrates are made of several sugar molecules. They provide long-lasting energy and stabilize your blood sugar, which boosts your endurance. Complex carbohydrates are also high in vitamins, minerals, and fiber.

GRILLED HAM AND CHEESE QUESADILLAS WITH TOMATO BISQUE

Carbohydrates, proteins, fats, and fiber work to keep our bodies running smoothly. You'll find all of them in this delicious and nutritious balanced meal.

PREP TIME | **15** MINUTES

COOK TIME | **30** MINUTES

MAKES | **4** 1-CUP SERVINGS OF SOUP AND **2** QUESADILLAS

Tools

- cutting board
- chef's knife
- saucepan
- measuring cups/spoons
- spoon
- large skillet
- spatula
- plate
- blender

Ingredients

For the soup:

- 1 small onion
- 1 clove garlic
- 1 15-ounce can crushed tomatoes
- 1 12-ounce can vegetable broth
- 1 teaspoon dried basil
- ½ cup half-and-half
- 1 teaspoon salt
- ½ teaspoon black pepper

For the quesadillas:

- 1 cup cheddar cheese, grated
- 6 slices deli ham
- 1 tablespoon olive oil
- 4 medium whole-wheat flour tortillas

1 Start the soup: Chop the onion into small pieces and mince the garlic. Place the onions and garlic, along with the tomatoes, broth, and basil, in a medium-sized saucepan on a stovetop with medium heat.

COACH'S TIP

Be careful when blending hot liquids. Hot steam builds pressure and can make the lid burst off, causing a big mess or burns. To prevent a cooking disaster, work in batches and only fill your blender half full. Always be careful when you take the lid off.

2 Stir to combine until it begins to bubble. Reduce the heat to medium-low and simmer for 10 minutes.

3 Meanwhile, chop the deli ham into bite-sized pieces. Set aside.

4 Place the oil in a large skillet over medium-high heat until it begins to sizzle.

5 Put one tortilla in the pan. Quickly and carefully sprinkle a quarter of the cheese on the tortilla, followed by half of the ham.

6 Add another quarter of the cheese, followed by a second tortilla, forming a sandwich. Allow to cook for about 1 to 2 minutes or until golden brown.

7 Using a spatula, carefully flip the quesadilla over and cook an additional 1 to 2 minutes.

8 Move the quesadilla from the pan to a plate and repeat steps 5 through 7 with the other two tortillas.

9 Cut the quesadillas into wedges and set aside while you finish the soup.

10 Carefully transfer the soup to a blender. Blend until smooth.

11 Return to the saucepan and add the half-and-half, salt, and pepper. Stir to combine.

12 Serve soup hot with quesadillas on the side.

STRAWBERRY-WALNUT CHICKEN SALAD

Go green with this sweet and savory salad! The mixed greens will give your vitamin A intake a boost.

PREP TIME	**15 MINUTES**
COOK TIME	**10 MINUTES**
MAKES	**2 CUPS**

Tools

- skillet
- measuring cups/ spoons
- plate
- spoon
- chef's knife
- cutting board
- 2 mixing bowls
- whisk
- 2 forks

Ingredients

- ¼ cup walnuts
- 1 tablespoon pure honey
- 1 pinch salt
- 3 strawberries
- 4 slices red onion
- 1½ cups mixed baby greens
- ½ cup rotisserie chicken, sliced

For the dressing:

- 4 tablespoons raspberry yogurt
- 1½ tablespoons red wine vinegar

ATHLETE NUTRITION

Vitamin A does more than keep your vision sharp. It also helps keep your immune system strong and prevents you from getting sick—so you can stay in the game!

CALL AN AUDIBLE

Not a nut fan? Make croutons instead! Cut a slice of bread into 1-inch cubes and place them on a baking sheet. Then drizzle 1 tablespoon of olive oil and sprinkle a pinch each of salt and pepper over the bread. Bake in the oven at 400°F for about 10 minutes or until golden brown.

1. In a skillet, combine the walnuts, honey, and salt. Place over medium-high heat, stirring frequently for about 2 to 3 minutes. Remove from heat and place the nuts on a plate to cool.

2. Cut the tops off the strawberries. Slice the strawberries into quarters and set aside.

3. Cut the onion into ¼-inch slices and set aside.

4. In a large bowl, combine the walnuts, strawberries, red onion, mixed greens, and chicken.

5. Make the dressing: In a small mixing bowl, whisk the yogurt and vinegar until smooth.

6. Drizzle the dressing over the salad and toss lightly with two forks to coat the salad. Serve in a bowl.

PITA PIZZA

Pizza on a game day? That's right! Start off with a pita instead of regular pizza crust and build your own tasty creation.

PREP TIME	**10** MINUTES
COOK TIME	**10** MINUTES
MAKES	**1** PIZZA

Tools

- chef's knife
- cutting board
- baking sheet
- pizza cutter

Ingredients

- 1 whole-wheat pita pocket
- 2 tablespoons pizza sauce
- ½ cup mozzarella cheese, grated
- your favorite pizza toppings, such as peppers, onions, mushrooms, ham, pepperoni, pineapple, or spinach

1 Preheat oven to 425°F.

2 Chop toppings into small pieces and set aside.

3 Spread pizza sauce on the pita pocket, followed by the cheese and toppings.

4 Place on a baking sheet and bake for 5 to 10 minutes, or until the cheese is bubbly and melted.

5 Remove from oven and slice into wedges with the pizza cutter. Allow to cool for 2 minutes. Serve hot.

COACH'S TIP

Choose your toppings wisely! By using a variety of ingredients, you can cover many food groups in your Pita Pizza.

BLT WRAP

Toast is so second-string! Use a tortilla to wrap up the classic ingredient trio before you head to the field.

PREP TIME	5 MINUTES
COOK TIME	10 MINUTES
MAKES	1 WRAP

Tools

- skillet
- tongs
- paper towels
- cutting board
- chef's knife
- small mixing bowl
- spoon
- toothpicks

Ingredients

- 2 slices bacon
- 1 small tomato
- 1 tablespoon ranch dressing
- 1 teaspoon Dijon mustard
- 1 10-inch whole-wheat flour tortilla
- 2 romaine lettuce leaves

CALL AN AUDIBLE

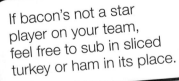

If bacon's not a star player on your team, feel free to sub in sliced turkey or ham in its place.

COACH'S TIP

Don't want to deal with splattering bacon on the stove? Cook your bacon in the oven on a baking sheet at 375°F for 15 to 20 minutes or until crispy. You can also cook the bacon in a microwave, although it won't get as crispy. On a microwave-safe plate, place two paper towels, the bacon strips, and then two more paper towels. The bacon should not overlap. Cook for about 2 minutes.

1   In a skillet over medium heat, cook the bacon until crisp— about 5 minutes on each side, using tongs to turn. Place on a paper towel to drain.

2   Cut the tomato into four slices and set aside.

3   Combine the ranch dressing and Dijon mustard in a small mixing bowl. Spread evenly on the tortilla.

4   Place the bacon on the tortilla, followed by the tomato and lettuce.

5   Roll up tightly and secure with toothpicks.

6   Slice in half and serve.

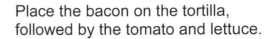

YOGURT PARFAIT

As you layer on your gear and uniform, dig through the fruit and yogurt layers of this parfait.

PREP TIME | **5 MINUTES**

MAKES | **1 PARFAIT**

Tools

- measuring cups
- cutting board
- chef's knife
- bowl
- spoon
- tall glass or parfait glass

Ingredients

- ¼ cup raspberries
- ¼ cup blueberries
- ¼ cup strawberries
- 1 cup your favorite yogurt
- ¼ cup Maple Nut Granola Cereal (see page 8)

1 Cut the strawberries into small pieces.

2 Mix the strawberries with the raspberries and blueberries in a bowl and set aside.

3 In a tall glass or parfait glass, add ⅓ cup of the yogurt, followed by ½ of the berry mixture. Repeat the layers, ending with the yogurt.

4 Top with granola and serve cold.

CALL AN AUDIBLE

You don't have to stick with just raspberries, blueberries, and strawberries. Mix and match your favorite fruits! Peaches, pineapple, and bananas can add a flavor twist to your parfait. If you want more crunch, mix some of the granola into the berry layers.

POPCORN TRAIL MIX

Mix it up and stay satisfied! For an energy boost that will help carry you through the game, grab a handful of this sweet and salty combo.

PREP TIME | **10** MINUTES

COOK TIME | **3** MINUTES

MAKES | **3** CUPS

Tools
• paper lunch bag
• measuring cups/spoons
• 2 mixing bowls

Ingredients
• ½ cup popping corn kernels
• 1 teaspoon coconut or olive oil
• ¼ teaspoon salt
• 1 cup roasted almonds
• 1 cup roasted peanuts
• ½ cup pumpkin seeds
• ½ cup semisweet chocolate chunks
• ½ cup raisins

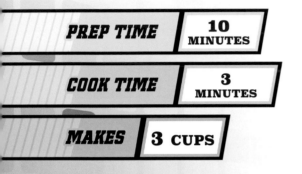

COACH'S TIP
Use single-serve zip-top bags to portion out the trail mix. Then you'll be set for a tasty snack every day of the week!

1 In a mixing bowl, combine the popping corn, oil, and salt. Stir until well coated.

2 Place the mixture into the paper lunch bag. Fold the top of the bag down two times to seal.

3 Place upright in a microwave. Cook on high for 2 minutes or until you no longer hear the corn popping for 1 or 2 seconds.

4 Allow to cool before opening the bag. Be careful—steam might escape out of the bag!

5 Combine the remaining ingredients and the popcorn in a second mixing bowl and stir well.

6 Transfer to an airtight container or large zip-top bag to store leftovers for up to one week.

VANILLA-ALMOND POWER BARS

The perfect treat to snack on during halftime! This granola bar will give you a boost of energy for the second half.

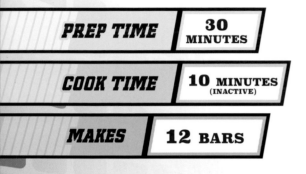

PREP TIME	30 MINUTES
COOK TIME	10 MINUTES (INACTIVE)
MAKES	12 BARS

Tools

- baking sheet
- parchment paper
- saucepan
- spoon
- mixing bowl
- knife

Ingredients

- ¼ cup canola oil
- ½ cup pure honey
- ¼ cup creamy peanut butter
- 2 teaspoons vanilla extract
- 2½ cups rolled oats
- 1 cup puffed brown rice cereal
- 1 cup chopped roasted almonds
- ½ cup chopped roasted peanuts
- ½ cup semisweet chocolate chips

1 Line the baking sheet with parchment paper and set aside.

2 In a medium-sized saucepan, combine the canola oil, honey, peanut butter, and vanilla extract over medium-high heat. Stir until it begins to simmer. Reduce heat to low and cook for about 3 minutes. Set aside.

3 In a large mixing bowl, combine the oats, rice cereal, almonds, peanuts, and chocolate chips.

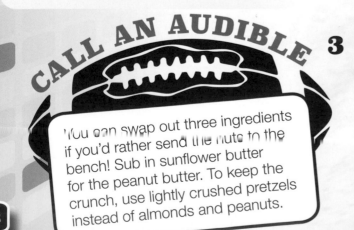

CALL AN AUDIBLE

You can swap out three ingredients if you'd rather send the nuts to the bench! Sub in sunflower butter for the peanut butter. To keep the crunch, use lightly crushed pretzels instead of almonds and peanuts.

4 Pour the mixture from the saucepan into the mixing bowl and stir until the oats are well coated.

5 Press the oats firmly into the baking sheet, packing the mixture tightly.

6 Refrigerate for at least an hour before cutting into bars. Store leftovers in an airtight container.

ATHLETE NUTRITION

Did you know a peanut isn't really a nut? It's a legume—in the same group as peas and beans. Peanuts and peanut butter are packed with lots of fiber and protein that serve as a source of fuel for your energy and muscles.

FRUIT KABOBS

An easy way to eat the rainbow! Share this fruity snack with your teammates for a burst of vitamin C.

PREP TIME | **15 MINUTES**

MAKES | **12 KABOBS**

Tools

- chef's knife
- cutting board
- 12 10-inch wooden skewers

Ingredients

- 24 strawberries
- 1 cup pineapple
- 1 cup cantaloupe
- 4 kiwis
- 1 cup blueberries
- 1 cup green grapes

ATHLETE NUTRITION

Feeling a slump at halftime? Fruit provides lots of energy through natural sugars. Fruit contains a lot of water, which helps prevent dehydration. The vitamin C helps your body recover during the game.

1. Start by prepping the fruit. Cut the tops off the strawberries. Cut the pineapple into 1-inch chunks. Cut the cantaloupe into ½-inch slices. Peel and slice the kiwi into ½-inch rounds.

2. Thread each skewer with the strawberries, cantaloupe, pineapple, kiwi, blueberries, and grapes. Get creative with your order of fruit!

3. Store in an airtight container or large zip-top bag in a refrigerator or cooler with ice packs until serving.

CALL AN AUDIBLE

Switch up the taste of your kabobs by changing the lineup of fruit. Mix and match the fruit from the ingredient list with watermelon chunks, orange segments, apples, honeydew, or red grapes.

MIXED BERRY ICE POPS

Your team won the game! Celebrate with delicious ice pops that will cool down you and your teammates.

PREP TIME	**10** MINUTES
COOK TIME	**4** HOURS (INACTIVE)
MAKES	**6** ICE POPS

Tools

- measuring cups/spoons
- blender
- ice pop form

Ingredients

- 2 cups low-fat plain yogurt
- 2 cups frozen mixed berries
- ½ cup 100 percent apple juice
- 1 teaspoon vanilla extract
- 2 teaspoons honey

CALL AN AUDIBLE

Sub out the flavors to get a new take on the ice pops. Try 2 cups frozen mangoes in place of berries and ½ cup 100 percent pineapple juice instead of apple juice for a tropical twist.

1 Place ingredients in a blender. Blend until smooth.

2 Pour the mixture evenly in an ice pop form.

3 Place the top of the form on and freeze for 4 hours before serving.

COACH'S TIP

Don't have an ice pop form? No problem! Make mini-ice pops by using an ice cube tray. Pour the mixture evenly into the cube cups and place in the freezer for 1 hour. Remove from the freezer and stick one toothpick into each cube. Put back in the freezer for 2 hours before serving.

CHOCOLATE-BANANA SMOOTHIE

Recover from a grueling game with this healthy alternative to a chocolate-banana milkshake.

PREP TIME | **10 MINUTES**

MAKES | **1 SMOOTHIE**

Tools
- cutting board
- chef's knife
- blender
- measuring cups/spoons

Ingredients
- 1 peeled banana, frozen
- 1 cup milk or almond milk
- ¼ cup low-fat plain yogurt
- 1 teaspoon vanilla extract
- 2 tablespoons unsweetened cocoa powder

ATHLETE NUTRITION

After a practice or game, it's important to replenish your body. Bananas contain simple carbohydrates, which are fast-acting sugars that go into recovery mode to rebuild and restore muscles. Other fruit to eat post-game are raisins, blueberries, grapes, watermelon, or pears.

1   Cut the banana into 1-inch rounds and place in the bottom of a blender.

2   Add the remaining ingredients.

3   Blend until smooth and serve immediately.

COACH'S TIP
The more ripe the banana, the sweeter it'll taste. Freeze bananas that are almost too ripe to eat. They'll last up to three months in the freezer and be ready for smoothies.

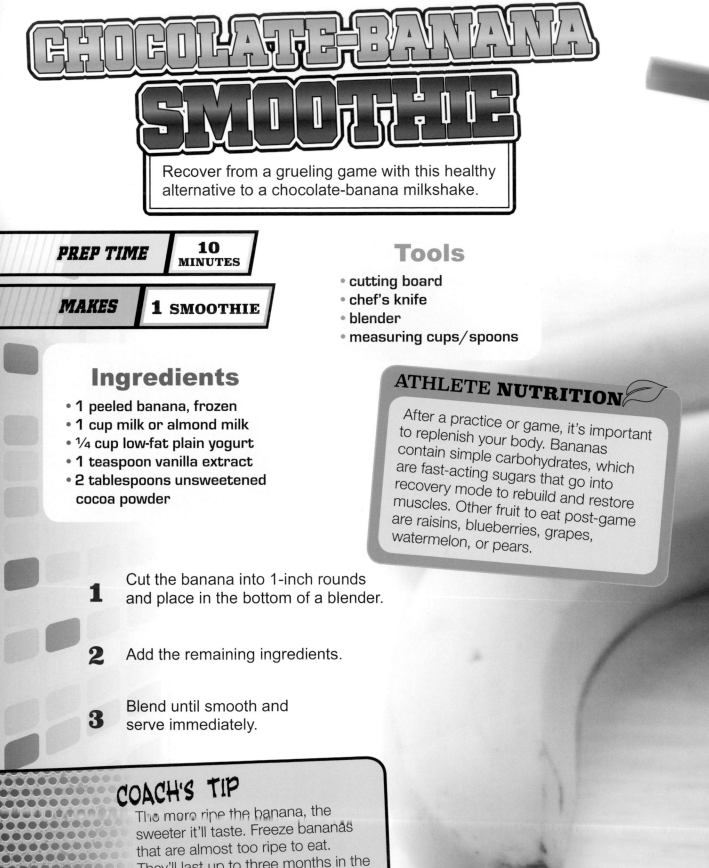

SOUTHWEST BLACK BEAN QUINOA BOWL

A satisfying post-game meal will restore your muscles with this south-of-the-border-inspired dish.

PREP TIME | **15** MINUTES

COOK TIME | **20** MINUTES

SERVES | **4** 2-CUP SERVINGS

Tools

- measuring cups/ spoons
- mesh strainer
- 2 saucepans
- cutting board
- chef's knife
- can opener
- skillet
- spoon

Ingredients

- 1 cup quinoa
- 2 cups water
- 1 red bell pepper
- 1 small red onion
- 1 tablespoon olive oil
- 1 teaspoon salt
- 2 teaspoons cumin
- 2 tablespoons lime juice
- ¼ teaspoon cayenne pepper
- 1 15-ounce can sweet corn, drained
- 1 15-ounce can black beans, drained

Garnishes:

- grated cheddar cheese, sour cream, salsa, diced avocado, chopped scallions, lime

1 Rinse the quinoa by placing in a mesh strainer and running cool water over it. Place in a saucepan with 2 cups water and bring to a boil.

2 Reduce the heat to low and cover. Cook for 15 to 20 minutes or until all the liquid is absorbed.

3 Meanwhile, slice the red pepper and onion into bite-sized pieces.

4 Heat oil in a skillet over medium heat. Add peppers and onions, along with salt, cumin, lime juice, and cayenne pepper. Cook 5 to 6 minutes or until slightly softened.

5 Add corn and black beans to the skillet. Stir until heated.

6 Combine the cooked quinoa with the veggies and stir to combine.

7 Serve in bowls and top with desired garnishes.

CALL AN AUDIBLE

Add some extra protein to your lineup! Shred 2 cups rotisserie chicken and add it to your quinoa bowl.

FISH TACOS

Fish is the ultimate athlete fuel. It provides a healthy balance of nutrition to help you recover faster and reduce soreness after the game.

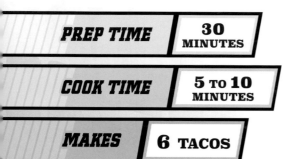

PREP TIME | **30 MINUTES**

COOK TIME | **5 TO 10 MINUTES**

MAKES | **6 TACOS**

Tools

- cutting board
- chef's knife
- 2 mixing bowls
- measuring spoons
- shallow baking dish
- skillet
- tongs

Ingredients

For the mango salsa:

- 1 mango
- 1 tomato
- ½ bunch cilantro
- 1 teaspoon salt
- ½ teaspoon pepper

For the tacos:

- 1 pound firm white fish, such as cod
- 1 tablespoon lime juice
- 1 tablespoon olive oil
- 1 tablespoon cumin
- 1 teaspoon salt
- ¼ teaspoon cayenne pepper
- 6 flour tortillas
- garnishes such as sour cream, grated cheese, and lettuce

1 Chop the mango and tomato into small pieces. Place in a mixing bowl.

2 Chop the cilantro finely and add to the bowl, followed by the salt and pepper.

3 Stir well and place in the refrigerator while you cook the fish.

CALL AN AUDIBLE

Not a fan of seafood? Replace the fish with chicken. For a vegetarian option, chop 1 pound of your favorite vegetables, such as bell peppers, onions, mushrooms, or zucchini, to use in place of the fish.

4 Cut the fish into 2-inch cubes and place in a shallow baking dish.

5 In a small mixing bowl, combine the lime juice, olive oil, cumin, salt, and cayenne pepper. Whisk well and pour over the fish. Allow to marinate for 5 minutes.

6 In a skillet over medium heat, add the fish and marinade. Using tongs, carefully turn the pieces over after 3 minutes. Then cook another 3 to 4 minutes or until cooked through.

7 Evenly place fish on six tortillas, followed by mango salsa and desired garnishes. Serve immediately.

COACH'S TIP

How do you know if your fish is done? Check by pressing your tongs gently against the piece of fish. If it flakes, it's done. If the meat is resistant, try cooking another minute or two and check again.

VEGETABLE PASTA

Bring on the whole wheat and pour on the veggies with this healthful pasta that will recharge you after the game.

PREP TIME	20 MINUTES
COOK TIME	20 MINUTES
MAKES	4 2-CUP SERVINGS

Tools

- stockpot
- colander
- cutting board
- chef's knife
- skillet
- can opener
- spoon
- tongs

Ingredients

- 1 tablespoon salt
- ½ pound whole-wheat pasta
- 1 yellow bell pepper
- 1 small onion
- ½ cup olive oil
- 1 cup frozen broccoli florets
- 3 teaspoons garlic, minced
- 1 15-ounce can fire-roasted tomatoes
- 1 teaspoon black pepper
- 1 tablespoon lemon juice
- ¼ cup Parmesan cheese, shaved

1 Fill a large stockpot ¾ full with water and add 1 tablespoon salt. Bring to a boil and cook pasta according to package directions. Drain and set aside.

2 Meanwhile, chop the bell pepper and onion into small pieces.

3 In a skillet, heat oil over medium heat and add zucchini and onions. Cook until slightly softened, stirring occasionally. Add broccoli and garlic and cook an additional 2 to 3 minutes.

4 Add tomatoes, pepper, and lemon juice. Reduce heat to low.

CALL AN AUDIBLE

For a little extra flavor in your pasta, add sliced summer squash in step 3 and sliced cherry tomatoes in step 5.

5 Combine the vegetables with the pasta in the skillet and toss together using tongs.

6 Serve in bowls and sprinkle with cheese.

ATHLETE NUTRITION

Whole-wheat grains are much better for you than their white counterparts. Whole-wheat pasta, for example, is made from flour that is not as processed, so more nutrient value is left for your body to consume. Eating whole wheat will provide you with plenty of B vitamins to keep up your energy.

SALMON WITH COUSCOUS SALAD

Your body needs to refuel after the game, and salmon—with couscous on the side—will bring you back up to speed.

PREP TIME | **10** MINUTES

COOK TIME | **1 HOUR 10 MINUTES** (1 HOUR INACTIVE)

MAKES | **4 SERVINGS**

Ingredients

For the couscous salad:

- 1 cup whole-wheat couscous
- 1½ cups vegetable broth
- 1 tablespoon olive oil
- 2 teaspoons garlic, minced
- 1 cup cherry tomatoes
- 1 small cucumber
- 1 small red onion
- 1 tablespoon fresh basil
- ¼ cup Parmesan cheese, grated
- ¼ teaspoon salt
- 1 teaspoon black pepper

For the salmon:

- 4 6-ounce salmon fillets
- 1 teaspoon salt
- 1 teaspoon black pepper
- 1 tablespoon olive oil

Tools

- saucepan
- measuring cups/ spoons
- fork
- cutting board
- chef's knife
- mixing bowl
- mixing spoon
- skillet
- tongs

1 First make the salad: In a saucepan, combine the couscous, vegetable broth, olive oil, and garlic. Bring to a boil and remove from heat. Then cover and allow to sit for 5 minutes or until the liquid is absorbed. Remove the lid and fluff the couscous with a fork by stirring it a few times. Allow to cool slightly.

2 Slice the tomatoes in half. Then cut the cucumber, onion, and basil into small pieces.

3 In a mixing bowl, combine the couscous, tomatoes, cucumber, onion, basil, Parmesan cheese, salt, and pepper. Stir well and place in a refrigerator to cool for an hour.

4 Evenly sprinkle the salt and pepper on both sides of the fish fillets.

5 In a skillet, heat oil over medium-high heat and add fillets. Cook about 4 to 5 minutes per side, or until the fish is cooked through.

6 Serve immediately with the couscous salad.

ATHLETE NUTRITION

Salmon is rich in omega-3 fatty acids. These acids help restore your muscles and increase future performance.

INSIDE-OUT CHICKEN PARMESAN

If you've mastered the other recipes, you're ready to prove you're a pro in the kitchen! Impress your friends by turning the classic chicken Parmesan dish inside-out!

PREP TIME	20 MINUTES
COOK TIME	30 MINUTES
MAKES	4 SERVINGS

Tools

- cutting board
- plastic wrap
- mallet
- 4 plates
- measuring spoons
- toothpicks
- shallow baking dish
- stockpot
- colander
- tongs

Ingredients

- 4 boneless, skinless chicken breasts
- 4 slices mozzarella cheese
- 4 tablespoons Parmesan cheese, grated
- 1 bunch fresh basil
- 1 teaspoon salt
- 1 teaspoon black pepper
- 2 tablespoons olive oil
- 1 28-ounce jar marinara sauce
- 1 pound whole-wheat pasta
- 1 tablespoon salt

1 Cover the cutting board with plastic wrap.

2 Put a chicken breast in the center of the cutting board. Then place another piece of plastic wrap over the chicken. Press it flat to make a seal.

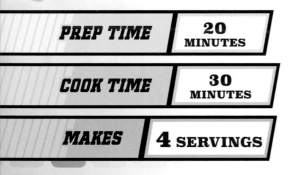

3 Using a mallet, gently pound the chicken breast until it is evenly flat and about ½-inch thick. Remove the chicken from the plastic and set on a clean plate.

4 Repeat steps 2 and 3 for the other three breasts. Then remove the plastic wrap from the cutting board.

5 Put one breast on the cutting board. In the center of the breast, place 1 slice of mozzarella cheese, 1 tablespoon of Parmesan cheese, and 4 basil leaves.

6 Fold the sides of the breast in and roll it up, like a burrito. Secure the chicken with toothpicks so it stays tightly rolled. Set aside.

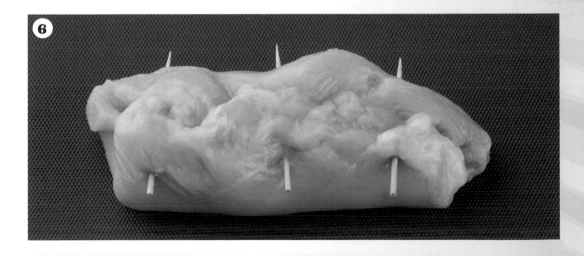

7 Repeat steps 5 and 6 for the other three breasts.

8 Preheat oven to 375ºF.

9 Place the chicken breasts evenly apart in the shallow baking dish. Sprinkle with salt and pepper. Bake in the oven for 35 to 40 minutes or until the chicken is cooked through.

10 Meanwhile, fill a stockpot 3/4 full of water and add 1 tablespoon salt. Bring to a boil.

11 Cook pasta according to package directions and drain in a colander.

12 Pour marinara sauce into the stockpot over medium heat. Bring to a simmer, then reduce heat to low.

13 When the chicken is done, carefully remove the toothpicks.

14 Add the pasta to the marinara sauce and toss carefully.

15 Serve by placing the pasta on a plate with the chicken breast on top.

READ MORE

Besel, Jen. *Baking Bliss! Baked Desserts to Make and Devour.* North Mankato, Minn.: Capstone Press, 2015.

Meachen Rau, Dana. *Sports Nutrition for Teen Athletes: Eat Right to Take Your Game to the Next Level.* Sports Illustrated Kids. North Mankato, Minn.: Capstone Press, 2012.

Pellman Good, Phyllis. *Fix-It and Forget-It Kids' Cookbook: 50 Favorite Recipes to Make in a Slow Cooker.* Intercourse, Pa.: Good Books, 2010.

Witherspoon, Jack. *Twist It Up: 60 Delicious Recipes from an Inspiring Young Chef.* San Francisco: Chronicle Books, 2011.

INTERNET SITES

FactHound offers a safe, fun way to find Internet sites related to this book. All of the sites on FactHound have been researched by our staff.

Here's all you do:

Visit *www.facthound.com*

Type in this code: 9781491421352

About the Author

Katrina Jorgensen is a graduate of Le Cordon Bleu College of Culinary Arts. She enjoys creating new recipes and sharing them with friends and family. She lives in Rochester, Minnesota, with her husband, Tony, and dog, Max.